The Lion's Heart series.

Let go and grow!

Kids and Emotional Freedom Techniques.

TANYA DE VILLIERS

ILLUSTRATED BY MARILIE FOUCHE

FOREWORDS

This book serves as a guide for parents, teachers, therapists and practitioners in facilitating the process of teaching children to let go. This book is specifically designed to condition children in letting go of negative emotions and bottled-up feelings. Children will gain new perspective and insight on being mindful and aware of emotions. The main purpose is to create an understanding that there is no benefit in keeping emotions bottled-up or handling them inappropriately.

Emotional Freedom Techniques (EFT) is one of many methods to successfully handle extreme emotions, limiting beliefs, addictions, learning barriers etc. The Lion's heart method is an adaptation of EFT and was specifically designed to be age appropriate and fun for young children.

Activities are incorporated to facilitate the learning process and activate both brain hemispheres, stimulate Kinesthesis functioning as well as incorporating Neuro Linguistic Programming (NLP). The Lion's heart method is not a quick fix and doesn't promise world peace, but it does promote self-, body and emotional awareness.

The process which unfolds in this book hold many benefits which include but are not limited to:
- Assist in teaching an essential life-skill.
- Builds a foundation for emotional intelligence and
- Being able to let go and GROW !

We all have emotions
and feelings,
that is so true.

Sometimes we laugh,

Sometimes we feel sad...

and that is good.

It is not bad to feel sad

and it is not bad to get mad.

It is how we act and what we do,
when we get mad or sad.

A Lion's heart always knows
what to do,

if you listen carefully you will
know what to do too.

Sometimes when we get mad, shocked or sad, we might do and say things that we are not supposed to.

Or we would do or say nothing and keep everything inside.

That is not good.

6

We need to let go of that
which makes us angry,
scared or sad.

The Lion's heart knows that your fingers can be used as a magic wand, that can help you be brave and to change that which is not supposed to be there.

Let the Lion's heart guide
and show you the way,
so that all the good feelings
get to stay.

Point with your finger which
feeling
you would like to take away.

I am.....

Angry

Lonely

Sad

Frustrated
Irritated

Worried

Feeling down

Feeling
sick

Now show me how BIG the feeling is?

Is it One, Two or Three?

Do you know why you are feeling the way you do?

What happened?
Do you know why this feeling would want to stay?

Say out loud how you are feeling and show it with your face.

Feeling down

Lonely

Feeling sick

I am ......

? ? ?
Worried

Frustrated Irritated

Angry

Sad

13

Now wiggle your nose and lightly tap it 3 times with your finger.

Jump up and down 3 times saying.

I am ......

Now tap lightly with your fingers
on top of your head

I am .....
because .....

Lightly tap with 3 fingers and tap between your eyebrows saying...

I am .....

Tap with your finger under your nose.

Now give a spin left and a spin right. Give a big shout with all your might.

17

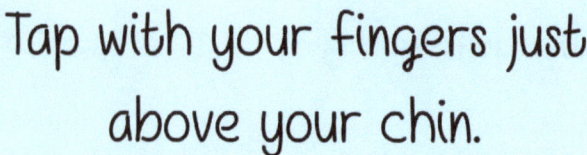

Tap with your fingers just
above your chin.

I am ......

Open your hand and tap on your chest.

Now put your hand on your heart
and take a deep breath in and
now softly blow everything
that is bothering you, out.

How big is this feeling now?
Or is it gone? Show me
with your hands.

Is it bigger...

...or smaller?

You can repeat the Lion's heart until the feeling is no longer there.

The Lion's heart can make good feelings stay.

Choose a feeling that you would like right now:

Brilliant/Smart

I am a winner

Joyful/Happy

I am beautiful

Superhero

Precious

The Lion's heart knows that you are all of these wonderful things, but you need to believe it! Take your magic finger and see the beautiful picture that makes you happy.

Would you like to paint the picture in your heart? Do you see it? Great! Now let's start painting.

Put on your pretend crown with both hands.

Now tapping lightly say :

" A king/ queen am I and a ruler of my own thoughts and emotions."

Tap lightly with three fingers
between the eyebrows and say:
"Beauty is all I see and beauty
is looking out for me."

Tap underneath the nose and say:
"Wonderful feelings fill my heart,
good is to come and wonders
will be done".

March like a soldier with your knees
high, touching each knee with
an opposite hand and count to 10.

1...2...3...4...5

6...7...8...9...10

Tap above the chin and give a
quick spin and say;
"Happy thoughts fill my mind".

Open your hand and tap on your chest.
Say:" I have the heart of a Lion and I know what to do".

Place your hand on your heart
and take a deep breath in
and slowly breathe out.

Give a big smile.

Let us look again at what we can do.

Put on crown and
tap lightly on top
of your head

Tap between
your eyebrows

Tap under
your nose

1...2...3...4...5

6...7...8...9...10

Walk like a soldier
and count to ten

Tap above your
chin and give a
quick spin

Tap on chest

Put your hand on
your heart.
Take a deep breath
in and out.
Now smile.

Now you have a Lion's heart too!

Use it, whenever you need to.

www.ingramcontent.com/pod-product-compliance
Lightning Source LLC
Chambersburg PA
CBHW050859290526
45792CB00002B/658